FORENSIC INVESTIGATIONS
OF THE
ANCIENT GREEKS

Heather C. Hudak

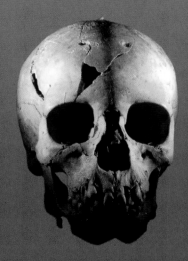

CRABTREE
PUBLISHING COMPANY
WWW.CRABTREEBOOKS.COM

Author: Heather C. Hudak

Editors: Sarah Eason, John Andrews,
    Petrice Custance, and Janine Deschenes

Proofreader and indexer: Wendy Scavuzzo

Editorial director: Kathy Middleton

Design: Paul Myerscough, Paul Oakley,
    and Jane McKenna

Cover design: Paul Myerscough

Photo research: Rachel Blount

**Production coordinator and
    Prepress technician:** Tammy McGarr

Print coordinator: Katherine Berti

Consultant: John Malam

Produced for Crabtree Publishing Company by
Calcium Creative Ltd.

Library and Archives Canada Cataloguing in Publication

Hudak, Heather C., 1975-, author
        Forensic investigations of the ancient Greeks /
Heather C. Hudak.

(Forensic footprints of ancient worlds)
Includes index.
Issued also in print and electronic formats.
ISBN 978-0-7787-4942-4 (hardcover).--
ISBN 978-0-7787-4955-4 (softcover).--
ISBN 978-1-4271-2115-8 (HTML)

        1. Greece--Antiquities--Juvenile literature. 2. Forensic
archaeology--Greece--Juvenile literature. 3. Archaeology and
history--Greece--Juvenile literature. I. Title.

DF78.H83 2018   j938.00909   C2018-902981-1
                                           C2018-902982-X

Library of Congress Cataloging-in-Publication Data

Names: Hudak, Heather C., 1975- author.
Title: Forensic investigations of the ancient Greeks /
    Heather C. Hudak.
Description: New York, N.Y. : Crabtree Publishing Company,
    2019. | Series: Forensic footprints of ancient worlds |
    Includes index.
Identifiers: LCCN 2018027912 (print) | LCCN 2018031060 (ebook) |
    ISBN 9781427121158 (Electronic) |
    ISBN 9780778749424 (hardcover) |
    ISBN 9780778749554 (pbk.)
Subjects: LCSH: Forensic archaeology--Greece--Juvenile
    literature. | Forensic anthropology--Greece--Juvenile literature.
    | Excavations (Archaeology)--Greece--Juvenile literature. |
    Greece--Civilization--To 146 B.C.--Juvenile literature. | Greece--
    Antiquities--Juvenile literature.
Classification: LCC CC79.F67 (ebook) |
LCC CC79.F67 H835 2019 (print) | DDC 938--dc23
LC record available at https://lccn.loc.gov/2018027912

Crabtree Publishing Company

www.crabtreebooks.com   1-800-387-7650

Printed in the U.S.A./092018/CG20180719

Published in Canada
Crabtree Publishing
616 Welland Ave.
St. Catharines, Ontario
L2M 5V6

Published in the United States
Crabtree Publishing
PMB 59051
350 Fifth Avenue, 59th Floor
New York, New York 10118

Published in the United Kingdom
Crabtree Publishing
Maritime House
Basin Road North, Hove
BN41 1WR

Published in Australia
Crabtree Publishing
3 Charles Street
Coburg North
VIC, 3058

CONTENTS

INVESTIGATING ANCIENT GREECE

About 2,500 years ago, the ancient Greeks created a **civilization** that changed how people saw the world. They took big steps in art, science, sports, and **politics**. Other civilizations admired the steps the ancient Greeks had taken and began to copy their ways of life.

The ancient Greeks lived in **mainland** Greece and on the Greek Islands. They also lived in the area now known as Turkey, and along the shores of the Mediterranean Sea. Their biggest city was called Athens. The ancient Greeks also settled in places as far away as North Africa, Italy, and France. They were mainly **seafarers** and **traders** who traveled in search of new lands, sharing their ways of life with people they met along the way.

Unlocking the Past

The ancient Greeks left behind many clues to their past. There are **artifacts** (objects from the past), such as sculptures, jewelry, and pottery. There are also building ruins, such as **temples** and **tombs** filled with bones. There is also a lot of written **evidence** that tells us what ancient Greece was like.

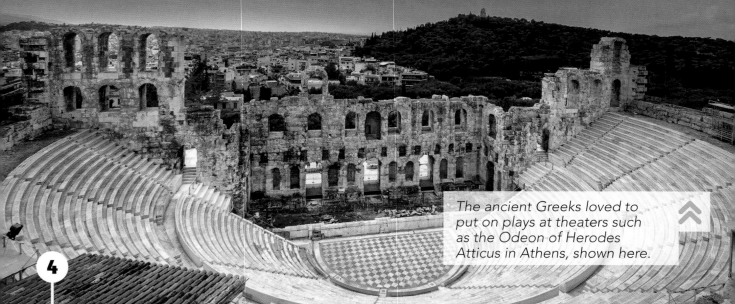

The ancient Greeks loved to put on plays at theaters such as the Odeon of Herodes Atticus in Athens, shown here.

This beautiful gold death mask was found in a tomb. It is known as "The Mask of Agamemnon." Artifacts as valuable as this tell us that important people were given impressive burials.

HOW SCIENCE SOLVED THE PAST:
FORENSIC FOOTPRINTS

To solve crimes, forensic scientists examine evidence from the places where crimes took place, called **crime scenes**. The **techniques** that they use to solve crimes are also used by people to solve mysteries about the past. **Archaeologists** and **anthropologists** study the clues, or forensic footprints, ancient people left behind to find out more about them. Archaeologists use forensic techniques to find out more about ancient buildings and **sites**. Anthropologists use forensic techniques to learn more about ancient peoples from their skeletons and the objects they left behind.

DID
You Know?

There could be as many as 750,000 ancient shipwrecks at the bottom of the Mediterranean Sea. Some date back more than 2,000 years. Each shipwreck contains artifacts such as jewelry, coins, statues, and pottery. Archaeologists use **forensic science** to examine the artifacts and learn more about the ancient Greeks. For example, chemical tests on objects made from a soft, gray metal called lead tell archaeologists where the lead was mined. This can help them figure out where the objects were made.

But how do we discover more about how the ancient Greeks looked and dressed, how they lived, and the jobs they did? How did they create such amazing cities and buildings? Is there a way to solve these ancient mysteries? Yes—with forensic science!

This was once an ancient Greek **merchant** ship. Forensic tests can tell us when the ship was built.

SOLVING PAST MYSTERIES

Forensic scientists can help police find a body in a recent crime scene and they can also find out where bodies were buried long ago. They dig up any items buried with the bodies, carefully make a note of them, and **preserve** them. They then use forensic science to find out more about the bodies and items.

Raiding the Remains

Just as forensic scientists study skeletons or bodies to solve mysteries about a crime, they study ancient remains to learn about people who lived long ago. Forensic scientists can carry out tests to find out when and why they died. Using the skulls of the dead, scientists can also use special **scanners** and computers to create a model of their faces.

So, what clues, or forensic footprints, did the Greeks leave behind and what can we learn from them? Let's follow their forensic footprint trail!

« Today, forensic technology such as this **virtual reality (VR)** headset (see "Did You Know?" opposite) allows us to step into the past and walk in the footsteps of the ancient Greeks.

DID
You Know?

Forensic scientists use cutting-edge forensic technology to recreate crimes scenes. Archaeologists are using the same technology to bring ancient Greece back to life! Using evidence from ancient sites, forensic scientists have built **three-dimensional (3-D)** pictures of ancient Greek cities. These images can then be seen through a VR headset and the viewer feels as though they are actually in ancient Greece! People can walk through the streets, touch the statues, and see what Greek cities were really like.

HOW SCIENCE SOLVED THE PAST:
MODELING MYSTERIES

We cannot visit the past, but we can model it. Forensic scientists use clues from ancient sites to figure out how the buildings that once stood there looked. For example, **foundations** in the ground hint at walls. Pieces of pottery lead to garbage sites. Using this information, archaeologists work on a computer to create a 3-D model of the site as it might once have been. This helps them learn how the buildings were made and what they might have been used for. Forensic scientists can also use clues from the past to make 3-D models of people who lived long ago. They study skulls and skeletons to figure out what a person looked like. They then use that information to create a 3-D model of the person.

⤊ Using computers, researchers can now create 3-D images of ancient buildings, such as the Parthenon in Athens, shown in the image above.

SKELETON SECRETS

A few miles south of Athens, in the ancient port city of Phaleron, archaeologists have dug up more than 1,500 skeletons. One group of 80 had their wrists tied together and were thrown facedown into a pit. Who were these people? What had they done to deserve this treatment? Forensic scientists are unlocking these mysteries using something called **DNA**.

DNA is found in every **cell** of all living things. It contains information about what the organism will look like, such as eye or hair color and height. Forensic scientists can find DNA in bones and teeth.

DID You Know?

More than 400 tiny skeletons were found at Phaleron in **ceramic** pots. Forensic tests confirmed that they were babies and young children. The pots show that these were ordinary Greeks who could not afford expensive burials. More DNA tests may be able to tell us how these children died.

The women in this painting are from an ancient people called the **Minoans** (see opposite). The Minoans are even older than the ancient Greeks. Thanks to DNA testing, we now know that the ancient Greeks **descended** partly from the Minoans.

Scientists **analyzed** the bones of the 80 skeletons and found that they were all young men. DNA tests showed that they were all healthy. So how had they died? Looking closely at the skulls it was clear that each young man had been killed by a blow to the head. But why were they killed?

Historians know that in 632 B.C.E., a man named Cylon had gathered an army and tried to take control of Athens. Cylon was a **nobleman** and also one of the first **Olympic champions**. Cylon's army was defeated, and he and his soldiers were **executed**. Could the skeletons in the pit at Phaleron be Cylon and his followers? Forensic scientists are using DNA tests to try to solve the mystery.

HOW SCIENCE SOLVED THE PAST:

ALL PART OF THE FAMILY?

For years, scientists have wondered who the **ancestors** of the ancient Greeks were. Were the ancient Greeks the descendants of the Minoan civilization that lived from about 2600 to 1100 B.C.E.? Or was it the **Mycenaean civilization** that lived between 1650 and 1200 B.C.E.? When forensic scientists tested DNA samples from Minoan and Mycenaean remains, they found that the two groups were actually closely **related**. So it seems the ancient Greeks were descended from a mixture of peoples.

When they find a skeleton, archaeologists dig it up carefully using special tools. They wear gloves to make sure that their own DNA does not get mixed up with DNA from the skeleton.

MASTER BUILDERS

Many ancient Greek cities had an **acropolis**, or "high city," in the center. It was a rocky hill where people could gather for safety if enemies attacked the city. The Acropolis of Athens has many ancient remains, including temples and statues. The most impressive temple is called the Parthenon.

Ready for Repair

Over the past 2,500 years, the Parthenon has been shaken by earthquakes, set on fire, and blown up. Parts of it have been taken to museums around the world. The Parthenon took less than ten years to build, but it has already taken more than 40 years for archaeologists and **engineers** to try to **restore** it! After so much damage, how can the temple ever be repaired? Forensic techniques, such as cutting-edge 3-D computer images, can help.

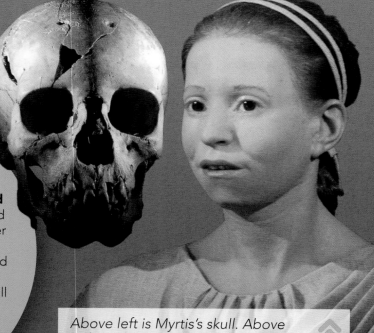

DID You Know?

Forensic scientists have **reconstructed** the face of an 11-year-old girl who lived in Athens around 430 B.C.E. They call her Myrtis, which was a common name in ancient Greece. Her remains were found during the building of a new subway station. The team scanned the girl's skull to create a 3-D picture of her face on a computer. DNA tests revealed that Myrtis died from **typhoid**, a disease that killed many people in Athens.

Above left is Myrtis's skull. Above right is the 3-D model of her that scientists created. The amazing reconstruction shows us how this young girl might have looked 2,500 years ago.

HOW SCIENCE SOLVED THE PAST:

WHERE DID THE STONES COME FROM?

The Parthenon is made mainly of a hard rock called **marble**, which becomes smooth and shiny when it is polished. The marble was dug out of **quarries** on Mount Pentelicus, about 10 miles (16 km) from Athens. The mountain had as many as 25 marble quarries, so which one produced the marble for the Parthenon? By comparing chemicals in the marble at the Parthenon with chemicals in marble from the different quarries, forensic scientists can figure out exactly where the marble used to build the Parthenon came from.

The police use computer graphics and 3-D models to recreate crime scenes and pieces of evidence. Now, archaeologists at the Acropolis Museum in Athens are using the same technology to help restore the Parthenon. First, they scan objects, such as sculptures and stone blocks, from different angles to make 3-D images on a computer. Those images can then be used to make **molds** that are the shape of the original building pieces. New pieces can then be made and used to replace damaged parts of the Parthenon.

It will take many years to rebuild the Parthenon, but thanks to 3-D modeling, we can now make sure that this incredible building will look as it did in ancient Greek times.

SEEING INTO THE STONES

One of the Parthenon's most amazing features is a stone **frieze** that runs 524 feet (160 m) all the way around the top of the temple. It shows hundreds of gods, heroes, women, and animals celebrating at a **festival**. Over time, parts of the sculpture have been damaged or removed and taken to museums around the world. Today, the frieze looks like natural stone. But did it look different during the time of the ancient Greeks? Forensic scientists are using **lasers** to find out!

A Big Cleanup

Greek archaeologists are using the latest laser technology to clean **pollution** from ancient buildings in Athens. Over the years, pollution has damaged the structure and color of many sculptures. Restorers use beams of **infrared** and **ultraviolet (UV)** light to clean the stone without damaging it. They tried the technique first on parts of the Parthenon frieze. Beneath the pollution, they found colors and decorations that had not been seen for centuries.

DID
You Know?

The ancient Greek civilization grew quickly and in just one small part of the world. How did the Greeks come up with so many amazing ideas, writings, and buildings in such a short time? By analyzing DNA from ancient Greek skeletons, scientists now know that around the time of the ancient Greeks many people migrated to Greece from eastern Europe and parts of Asia. They may have brought with them new ideas that helped the ancient Greek civilization grow.

« This is a section of the Parthenon frieze. It is held in the British Museum in London, England. Restorers have worked on the sculpture to clean it and reveal its amazing detail.

HOW SCIENCE SOLVED THE PAST:

THE MEANINGS OF COLOR

From 1885 to 1889, archaeologists dug deep beneath the layers of soil and stone that had built up around the Acropolis. They found many artifacts dating back to 480 B.C.E. that still had traces of paint. Now, scientists can use state-of-the-art forensic machines called spectrometers to "see" the colors in more detail. A spectrometer can break down the chemicals in an object so that each chemical can be analyzed. So far, archaeologists have learned the four main colors used on the Parthenon were white, red, black, and a yellowish-brown color called **ochre**. To the ancient Greeks, these colors represented the four **elements** of the universe—water, fire, earth, and air.

*Paint on artifacts wears away over many years, but tiny traces may be left behind. Using a **spectrometer**, scientists can use these traces to discover what colors artifacts were painted thousands of years ago.*

Scientists studying ancient Greek sculptures such as the one shown right, are learning that they were once colored with bright paints. The sculpture shown left is of the Greek goddess Athena. It shows how the Greeks may have painted her in ancient times.

LONG LOST CITIES

For more than 200 years, archaeologists have known about ancient ruins in the hills of Vlochós, located about 186 miles (300 km) north of Athens. But they pretty much ignored the site, thinking it was just a small country settlement. Were they wrong? Was there something that they could not see?

In 2016, researchers stumbled across the ruins of a few gates, walls, and towers on a nearby hill and realized there may be more to Vlochós than everyone thought. Digging into the earth to test their theory would take a lot of time and money, so instead, they used forensic science to see beneath the ground.

HOW SCIENCE SOLVED THE PAST:

ANCIENT TOWN PLANNING

About an hour from Vlochós is the site of the ancient city of Pherae. People lived in the city from around 3,000 B.C.E. to 1 C.E., when it was **abandoned**. Later, the town of Velestino was built on top of part of the ancient city. So how do archaeologists know exactly where the buildings of Pherae are? Images taken by **satellites** in space can show the outlines of buildings unseen on the ground. They revealed a well-planned network of streets and city blocks beneath Velestino.

From satellite images taken in space, we can see ancient sites in detail. This helps us discover information that would be impossible to learn from the ground.

*A **ground-penetrating radar (GPR)** device builds up a 3-D picture of hidden buildings underground. From these images, we can*

Using GPR, researchers discovered a 2,500-year-old lost city under the earth at Vlochós. Police use GPR to find human remains and other objects that can act as clues to help solve crimes. Researchers in Vlochós used GPR to send radar signals into the earth. Those signals bounced off objects and buildings underground, creating a picture of a forgotten ancient Greek city that covered nearly 100 acres (40 hectares), or 75 football fields! It included an entire town square and a network of streets.

DID You Know?

On the Italian island of Sicily, archaeologists have found an ancient Greek city called Selinunte. Everyone who lived in Selinunte was killed or taken as slaves by North African invaders in the 5th century B.C.E. Then, strong winds gradually covered the city in sand and dirt, preserving much of it underground. Archaeologists have even found the remains of half-eaten food! They are using forensic techniques to analyze the artifacts and learn more about how the people of Selinunte lived.

The people of Selinunte would have worshiped at this temple. Scientists hope to learn much more about them through forensic analysis of their ancient city.

TOMBS OF HEROES?

In 2012, archaeologists discovered a huge tomb on a hill called Kasta in northern Greece. Inside the tomb, they found many artifacts dating back to the time of Alexander the Great, a king who lived during the 4th century B.C.E. Researchers were excited—they may have found the tomb of Alexander or, if not, another important person from ancient times.

Dating Game

Inside the tomb, archaeologists found 550 bone fragments in a large stone coffin. From these fragments, they created 157 complete bones belonging to five different people. To learn the age and sex of the people, scientists used DNA analysis and a technique called **carbon dating**. All living things, including humans, have a substance called carbon in their bodies, even after they die.

The tomb at Kasta is a very important site for archaeologists. To learn more about it, they have recreated the tomb as a 3-D model. It shows the different chambers, or rooms, inside the tomb.

Many facinating artifacts were buried inside Philip II's tomb. This amazing gold chest and crown are two of them.

HOW SCIENCE SOLVED THE PAST:

A KING IS FOUND

About 100 miles (160 km) away from Kasta is another impressive tomb. No one knew for sure whose remains were in the tomb until forensic researchers used powerful **X-rays** and **microscopes** to look at 350 bone fragments found inside. On one leg bone piece, they found evidence of an injury, probably caused in battle by a **lance**. Historians knew that Philip II, Alexander the Great's father, had been lanced in the knee. DNA testing showed the man was about 45 when buried—about the same age Philip was when he died. This was the tomb of Philip II!

This ancient Greek coin shows the face of Philip II. From artifacts like this, we can learn more about what important people in the past looked like.

Carbon **decays** at a set rate, so forensic scientists can figure out how old a bone is by seeing how much carbon it has left. Using these tests, scientists discovered who four of the bodies belonged to: a woman of 60, two men aged 35–45, and a baby. The name of Alexander the Great's best friend, Hephaestion, has been found carved at the tomb. Does the fifth body belong to Hephaestion? Is this his tomb? Forensic science may help us find out.

DID You Know?

It was a dangerous business being a king in the ancient world! Forensic studies of Philip II's bones have shown his leg injury left him **lame**. His right collar bone was shattered by a lance, his left hand had been slashed, perhaps by a sword, and he was blinded in one eye by an arrow.

TRACKING THE RACES

Olympia was one of the most important places in ancient Greece. It was the home of the ancient **Olympic Games**, which began in 776 B.C.E. Horse and **chariot** races took place in the Hippodrome, a huge **stadium** about 2,000 feet (610 m) long and 650 feet (198 m) wide. For many years, archaeologists thought that the Hippodrome had been completely destroyed. Then, in 2008, they found its remains! So how did archaeologists locate the Hippodrome? They used forensic techniques, such as **radar** waves and measuring **magnetic fields**, to search beneath the soil.

HOW SCIENCE SOLVED THE PAST:

DATING THE TEMPLE

The Temple of Hera at Olympia is one of the best-preserved Greek temples. At first, archaeologists thought the temple dated back to 1100 B.C.E., but forensic scientists have used **photogrammetry** to find a more accurate date. This technique joins together thousands of **digital** photographs on a computer to make a very accurate 3-D image. Archaeologists used 4,350 digital photographs of the Temple of Hera to create 3-D models of exactly how it once looked. Building experts could tell from the design and style of the temple that it dated back to around 600 B.C.E.

The ancient Greeks raced chariots (such as the one shown at left) around the Hippodrome. These races would have been fast-paced and dangerous!

A magnetic field is a force that surrounds some objects, such as iron, steel, brick, and rock. The force can be strong or weak. Archaeologists use machines that can pick up these forces and figure out which objects or substances they come from. At Olympia, scientists found ditches and walls buried under the earth that matched the size of the Hippodrome. They also used GPR and satellite images to figure out where the Hippodrome was and what it looked like.

Viewed from the air today, we can see the layout of Olympia in clear detail. This image was taken by a drone. The site was hit by a **tsunami** in ancient Greek times.

DID
You Know?

A natural disaster buried Olympia under as much as 26 feet (8 m) of sand and dirt. Until recently, scientists thought an earthquake and floods destroyed Olympia. After using forensic scans of the ground and layout of Olympia, scientists believe that such a huge amount of sand and mud must have been carried by another incredibly powerful force of nature—a tsunami. Scientists have also found the remains of creatures at Olympia that could have only lived in the sea, many miles away!

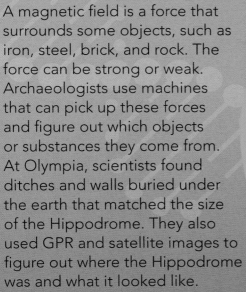

BURIED BY A VOLCANO

In the 1960s, archaeologists found the remains of an ancient town called Akrotiri on the Greek island of Santorini. About 4,000 years ago, disaster struck Akrotiri when earthquakes and a volcano destroyed the town and forced its people to flee for their lives. For years, archaeologists have tried to figure out exactly when this happened and who these people were. Thanks to forensic technology, archaeologists can now find the answers. Scientists must act fast, though. Earthquakes and the nearby volcano could destroy the ancient ruins all over again.

Surprises Underground

When the volcano **erupted**, a thick layer of dust, called **ash**, covered Akrotiri. This preserved many of the town's buildings. The preserved buildings allowed archaeologists to see just how the ancient Greeks in the town had lived.

Akrotiri would have been an impressive town in ancient times. These are its remains. You can almost imagine the ancient Greeks walking around its streets!

Just like crime scene investigators use 3-D laser scanners to create images of crime scenes, archaeologists used lasers to scan the buildings of Akrotiri. This produced digital images of what Akrotiri looked like in ancient times. Using GPR, researchers also sent signals underground to find the parts of Akrotiri that lie hidden beneath the earth. The amazing finds included a complicated **drainage system**, multistory buildings, wall paintings, furniture, and other artifacts. These clues to the past proved that Akrotiri was once a rich city and port.

DID
You Know?

There are no skeletons at Akrotiri. So where did the people go? It could be the local people knew they were in danger and escaped the island before the volcano erupted. Some scientists think that forensic investigations outside of Akrotiri may reveal evidence of human remains. They believe some people may have tried to run to higher ground to get away from volcanic ash and deadly gases rather than leave the island.

HOW SCIENCE SOLVED THE PAST:

EXTENDING AN OLIVE BRANCH

Some scientists believe an olive branch from Akrotiri covered in volcanic ash could prove exactly when the city was destroyed. They used carbon dating to analyze the branch and found the olive tree must have died between 1627 and 1600 B.C.E., when the volcano erupted. Until forensic research like this, experts thought that Akrotiri was destroyed around 100 to 150 years earlier.

This wall painting of two boys boxing was found in Akrotiri. Scientists must race against time to preserve artifacts like this one before another natural disaster hits Santorini.

PUTTING ISTHMIA ON THE MAP

Isthmia was an important gathering place for the ancient Greeks. It had its own sports festival and was also a place where kings such as Alexander the Great and other important Greek leaders met. However, Isthmia is not as well known as many other ancient sites in Greece. What made Isthmia such a special place? The latest forensic techniques help archaeologists reveal more about Isthmia—with no digging!

Digital Dig

Forensic scientists often make digital versions of clues and paperwork from old crime scenes to share with other investigators. In the same way, researchers at Isthmia are making digital versions of old photos, journals, and other records and sharing them on the Internet. By doing a "digital dig," researchers around the world can make new discoveries about Isthmia without ever visiting the site! A recent researcher looking at digital satellite images has even discovered a huge exercise area, called a **gymnasium**, about 590 feet (180 m) long and 230 feet (70 m) wide.

HOW SCIENCE SOLVED THE PAST:

CITY OF HONEY?

Researchers found pottery at Isthmia that looked a lot like beehives used today on Greek islands. Could they prove that the ancient people of Isthmia were beekeepers? Forensic scientists analyzed the chemicals on **residue** stuck to pieces of pottery and found evidence of **beeswax**. It looks like ancient Isthmians really did enjoy their honey!

The ancient Greeks did not have sugar. They used honey, instead, to sweeten their foods.

Researchers have found even more information about Isthmia by using **drones** and **Global Positioning Systems (GPS)**. Drones are small, unmanned aircraft that fly over a site and take pictures and video from above. GPS uses signals from satellites to find evidence of buildings that cannot be seen on the ground. These two technologies have given archaeologists the first complete 3-D map of Isthmia.

Modern forensic technology allows researchers to collect information at a rate that was impossible years ago. By flying drones over ancient sites, we can take photos of them quickly and easily.

DID
You Know?

Drones flying over the ruins of Aphrodisias, an ancient Greek city in Turkey that dates back to the 1st century B.C.E., gathered as much information in just a few hours as researchers would have captured in months of hands-on work. The drones took images of the area that were used to create a 3-D model of the ruins. From this, archaeologists could measure the size of buildings and even the width of ancient streets.

This photo of Isthmia was taken by a drone. From it, researchers can see the remains of the city's buildings. This helps them figure out what life might have been like in the city thousands of years ago.

CAVE PEOPLE

The Cave of Theopetra in northern Greece is one of the oldest archaeological sites in Greece. The massive cave was formed between 137 and 65 million years ago! Its location close to the Lithaios River made it the perfect place for ancient people to live. They had clean drinking water without needing to walk for miles to find it. But who were these ancient cave dwellers? Researchers are piecing the puzzle together with forensic science.

Ancient Greek pots such as this one hold lots of forensic clues. Scientists can test the tiniest bit of remains found inside the pots to discover what they are and what they may have been used for.

The Cave of Theopetra lies within this giant rocky area. The forensic clues inside the cave are helping scientists learn more about the people who lived in it long ago.

Cave People

Archaeologists found ancient remains, such as human bones and footprints, inside the cave. Using DNA tests, they found out that people lived in the cave from 135,000 to 4,000 B.C.E. Shepherds still used the cave up to the 1950s! Archaeologists are using their findings to help them learn how present-day humans **evolved** from early humans.

Early Builders

Archaeologists also used a forensic technique called **optical dating** on the remains of a stone wall that had once partly covered the entrance to the cave. Optical dating can find the age of an object from the amount of **energy** it gives off. Scientists figured out that the wall was an incredible 23,000 years old, making it the oldest-known human-made structure on Earth! Historians believe the wall was likely built to keep out the cold.

Researchers have built bridges and platforms inside the Cave of Theopetra. This allows them to move around the cave and study it without causing damage.

HOW SCIENCE SOLVED THE PAST:

WHO TOOK ALL THE BONES?

Archaeologists have found no bones in the central area of the Cave of Theopetra. At first, they thought no one had lived in that part of the cave—but they were wrong. Forensic scientists tested the soil on the cave floor. They found tiny traces of bone. Thousands of years of flooding in the cave had broken the bones down into pieces that could only be seen with a powerful microscope.

Even the tiniest traces of human remains can today be studied and analyzed using forensic techniques.

RISING FROM THE WATERS

The ancient town of Epidaurus was one of the most popular healing centers in ancient Greece. It was built in honor of Asclepius, the Greek god of healing. Its remains include a temple and the best-preserved ancient Greek theater. However, many more ancient discoveries lie at the bottom of the sea near Epidaurus. After a volcano erupted in 258 B.C.E., parts of the city's ancient harbor sunk into the ocean. What can the ruins tell us about the past? Archaeologists are using forensic science to find out!

DID You Know?

Archaeologists have found a sunken Greek city that is 5,000 years old! Pavlopetri is the oldest submerged city in the Mediterranean Sea. It disappeared under the sea around 1,000 years ago after an earthquake. Scientists are using cutting-edge forensic technology, including robot-operated cameras, to create a 3-D map of the underwater buildings and other remains. Computer-generated imagery (CGI), which creates the special effects we see in movies, is also being used to bring artifacts, such as large pottery jars, to life.

Just a few remains of the city of Pavlopetri can be seen above water today. The rest of this amazing ancient site lies hidden beneath the waves.

HOW SCIENCE SOLVED THE PAST:

BATTLE STATIONS!

In 480 B.C.E., a few hundred Greek warships defeated 1,200 ships from **Persia** in a big sea battle near Athens. It was called the Battle of Salamis. For a long time, no one knew where the Greeks had gathered their ships for the fight. Now, using forensic techniques such as drone photography and 3-D mapping, scientists have found **fortifications**, walls, and a port in Ampelakia Bay on the island of Salamis. They have also dated broken jugs and coins found at the site to the time of the battle. All the evidence suggests Ampelakia Bay is where the Greeks got ready to fight.

Archaeologists need to act fast if they want to learn more about the sunken harbor. It is under threat from natural forces and human activities, such as building and even theft. Divers use 3-D cameras to take pictures of the ancient ruins underwater. Drones take images of the site from above the sea. The information is then pieced together to create a 3-D map of the ruins. The finds from the sunken harbor of Epidaurus include a Roman **villa** and other Roman artifacts. This shows that Epidaurus traded with people from all over the Mediterranean.

This painting shows the fierce battle between the Persians and the ancient Greeks.

Warships such as this one were used by the ancient Greeks at the Battle of Salamis. It took more than 150 men to row each ship. Soldiers fought from a flat platform above.

FORENSIC FUTURE

Archaeologists have uncovered many clues about how the ancient Greeks lived, but we may never know all the details. With the help of forensic science, we can learn more today than ever before. Forensic techniques allow us to look for lost cities under the earth using GPR and satellites. We can date ancient artifacts using carbon samples, and identify human remains with DNA analysis. Archaeologists use this hard evidence to develop new ideas about the past and answer questions that have puzzled people for years.

New forensic technology that archaeologists can use to solve ancient mysteries is being developed all the time. Who knows what future technologies will uncover about the past? As we fit together more pieces of the puzzle, our picture of ancient Greece is becoming clearer all the time.

Forensic science may prove that the ancient Greeks were building pyramids such as the Hellinikon (above) at the same time as the ancient Egyptians.

DID You Know?

The ancient Egyptians were not the only ones to have **pyramids**. There are 16 pyramids in Greece. The most famous is the Hellinikon pyramid in Argos. No one knows why the pyramid was built or what it was used for. Was it a tomb? Was it used as a place of worship or for looking at the stars? Archaeologists are using forensic science, such as optical dating, to try to solve the mystery. Some findings suggest the Hellinikon may date back as far as 2720 B.C.E., which would make it as old as the oldest pyramids in Egypt!

CAN FORENSICS SOLVE...?

Here are two of the great still-unsolved mysteries about ancient Greece. Forensic scientists are using forensic footprints to try to solve these mysteries, too!

Disappearing Act

The Mycenaean civilization was one of the most powerful in ancient Greece. From around 1650 B.C.E., the Mycenaeans created a vast trade network across Italy, Turkey, and Egypt. The wealthy civilization built grand palaces, fought many wars, and developed a strong culture. Then, around 1200 B.C.E., the Mycenaeans suddenly vanished. What happened to the civilization? What made it collapse? Forensic scientists are using DNA analysis on skeletons and artifacts found in tombs and other ruins to tell us more about the collapse of the Mycenaeans.

Better Builders?

The ancient Greeks built the Parthenon in Athens in just eight or nine years. Even with all the technology we have today, modern builders would find it difficult to do the same. How did ancient Greek craftsmen manage to build and decorate the temple so quickly? Forensic scientists are using techniques such as laser scanning and 3-D imaging to find out. They hope to figure out ancient building methods and identify tools that have been lost over time. They plan to use the same methods to recreate the missing and damaged Parthenon pieces.

Once we discover how the ancient Greeks built buildings such as the Parthenon so quickly, we may be able to use their supersmart building techniques, too.

GLOSSARY

Please note: Some **bold-faced** words are defined where they appear in the book.

abandoned Left and never returned to

analyzed Looked at carefully

ancestors Relatives who died long ago

anthropologists Experts who study who ancient people were, how they lived, and where they came from

archaeologists Experts who study where ancient people lived and the things they left behind

beeswax Substance made by bees

cell The basic building block of all living things

ceramic A kind of pottery made from baked clay

chariot A vehicle with two wheels pulled by horses that was used in races and in battle

civilization A settled and stable community in which people live together peacefully and use systems such as writing to communicate

decays Rots and breaks down

descended Is related to a person or people who lived in the past

digital Information, such as a picture, that can be seen on a computer

drainage system The way that water is taken to a building or away from it

elements The four substances—air, earth, fire, and water—that ancient people believed made up the universe

energy Power that can be taken from something and used

engineers People who design and build complicated things, such as bridges and harbors

erupted Burst out in a sudden explosion

evidence Facts and information that tell us if something is true

evolved Developed over time

executed Killed for committing a crime

festival A special event where people celebrate

forensic science The use of scientific methods and techniques to find clues about crimes or the past

fortifications Buildings that are put up to protect something

foundations Solid structures that support a building from underneath

frieze A band used for decoration that runs around a building

infrared A kind of light that cannot be seen

lame Unable to walk properly because of illness or injury

lance A spear carried by a soldier on horseback

lasers Narrow, concentrated beams of light

magnetic fields Areas around objects where magnetic forces can be detected

mainland A large area of land that does not include islands

merchant A person who buys and sells products in large amounts, especially by trading

microscopes Devices used to see objects that are too small to be seen by the naked eye

Minoans An ancient civilization that lived on Crete and other Greek islands from around 2600 to 1100 B.C.E.

molds Hollow objects in which other objects can be shaped

Mycenaean civilization An ancient people that lived in Greece from around 1650 to 1200 B.C.E.

nobleman A man with a high rank

Olympic champions Winners of events held at the sports festival at Olympia in ancient Greece

Olympic Games Ancient sports festival that took place in Olympia every four years from 776 B.C.E. to 394 C.E.

optical dating Figuring out the age of an object from the amount of light it gives off

Persia A country in southwest Asia that was a rival to the ancient Greeks

politics The work of governing a city or country

pollution Substances that are harmful or damaging

preserve Make sure something stays the same

pyramids Large structures built with a square base and four triangular sides meeting at a point at the top

quarries Large, deep pits where stone and other materials are dug out

reconstructed Put together again to make something as it was originally

related In the same family

residue The leftovers of a liquid that has dried up

restore Return to a former condition or state

satellites Machines in space that collect information or are used for communication

scanners Special machines that look at something carefully

seafarers People who work on ships

sites Places where something is or was

stadium A place where races took place in ancient Greece

techniques Methods of doing particular tasks

temples Buildings where people go to worship their god or gods

three-dimensional (3-D) Having or appearing to have length, width, and depth

tombs Buildings in which dead bodies are kept

traders People who buy and sell goods

tsunami A high wave cause by an earthquake

ultraviolet (UV) A kind of light that cannot be seen

villa A large house

virtual reality (VR) A 3-D, computer-generated world that can be explored by a person

X-rays Waves of energy that can be used to create pictures of the inside of an object

LEARNING MORE

Books

Edwards, Roberta. *Where Is the Parthenon?* Penguin Workshop, 2016.

Kelly, Mina. *Amazing Pictures and Facts About Ancient Greece.* CreateSpace Independent Publishing Platform, 2017.

Malam, John. *Ancient Greece Inside Out* (Inside Out). Crabtree Publishing Company, 2017.

Ohlin, Nancy. *Blast Back! Ancient Greece.* Little bee books, 2016.

Websites

www.dkfindout.com/uk/history/ancient-greece
Take the Ancient Greece quiz and discover much more about the ancient Greeks with DK findout!

www.historyforkids.net/ancient-greece.html
Explore lots of different things about the ancient Greeks, including daily life, science, food, and clothes.

www.natgeokids.com/za/discover/history/greece/10-facts-about-the-ancient-greeks/#!/register
Discover ten cool facts about ancient Greece.

www.pbs.org/wgbh/nova/ancient/restoring-parthenon.html
See how experts are restoring the Parthenon in Athens.

INDEX

About the Author

Heather C. Hudak has written hundreds of children's books about all kinds of topics. She loves traveling the world, learning about new cultures, and sharing her experiences on her blog www.wanderlustwayfarer.com.